D0229156

Books should be returned on or before the
last date stamped below

04 AUG 2004   2 0 F   2006
25 SEP 2004   1 0 SEP 2011
                     3 1 MAR 2010
22 NOV 2004   2 6 SEP 2011
                                        2011
27 NOV 2004   1 4 NOV 2011   2 0 FEB 2014
2 0 DEC 2004   2 6 AUG 2013   - 7 MAY 2014
5 DEC 2005   1 7 JUN 2014
                     1 6 SEP 2013 2   OCT 2014
17 OCT 2011   1 3 JUN 2015
                                     2 5 JUL 2015

ABERDEENSHIRE LIBRARY
AND INFORMATION SERVICE
MELD Parker, Steve   UM

Seal : habitats,
life cycles,
food chains,
              J599.
              79
1221895

A L I S
1221895

NATURAL WORLD

SEAL

HABITATS • LIFE CYCLES • FOOD CHAINS • THREATS

Steve Parker

HODDER
Wayland

an imprint of Hodder
Children's Books

WWF®

Produced in Association with WWF-UK

NATURAL WORLD

Black Rhino • Cheetah • Chimpanzee • Crocodile • Dolphin • Elephant
Giant Panda • Giraffe • Golden Eagle • Gorilla • Great White Shark
Grizzly Bear • Hippopotamus • Kangaroo • Killer Whale • Koala • Leopard
Lion • Moose • Orangutan • Penguin • Polar Bear • Seal • Tiger • Wolf • Zebra

Produced for Hodder Wayland by
Roger Coote Publishing
Gissing's Farm, Fressingfield
Suffolk IP21 5SH, UK

Produced in association with WWF-UK.
WWF-UK registered charity number
1081247. A company limited by guarantee
number 4016725. Panda device © 1986 WWF.
® WWF registered trademark owner.

Cover: An inquisitive common seal studies the camera.
Title page: Every common seal has different spots and markings.
Contents page: Seals have thick body fur and a layer of fat under
the skin to keep them warm.
Index page: The leopard seal is a large, powerful seal that lives in
the oceans around Antarctica.

JS99.79
1221895

Published in Great Britain in 2003 by Hodder Wayland,
an imprint of Hodder Children's Books
Text copyright © 2003 Hodder Wayland
Volume copyright © 2003 Hodder Wayland

Editor: Angela Wilkes
Series editor: Victoria Brooker
Designer: Sarah Crouch

All rights reserved. No part of this publication may be
reproduced, stored in a retrieval system, or transmitted,
in any form or by any means without the prior written
permission of the publisher, nor be otherwise circulated
in any form of binding or cover other than that in
which it is published and without a similar condition
being imposed on the subsequent purchaser.

British Library Cataloguing in Publication Data
Parker, Steve, 1952-
  Seal. - (Natural world)
  1.Seals (Animals) - Juvenile literature
  I.Title
  599.7'9

ISBN 0 7502 4382 1

Printed and bound by G. Canale & C.S.p.A., Turin, Italy

Hodder Children's Books
A division of Hodder Headline Limited
338 Euston Road, London NW1 3BH

Picture acknowledgements
Bruce Coleman Collection 3 (Charles and Sandra
Hood), 9 (Hans Reinhard), 36 (Jim Watt); *FLPA* front
cover (Minden Pictures), 10 (H D Brandl), 11 (Tony
Hamblin), 15 (Leeson/Sunset), 43 (F di Domenico/
Panda Photo), 44 top (H D Brandl), 44 middle (Tony
Hamblin), 44 bottom (Leeson/Sunset); Nature Picture
Library 18 (Jeff Foott), 20 (Doug Wechsler), 22
(Florian Graner), 23 (Doug Allan), 28 (Mike Wilkes),
29 (Doug Allan), 34 (Thomas D Mangelsen), 35 (Jeff
Foott), 37 (Jeff Rotman), 38 (Sue Flood), 41 (Lynn
Stone), 45 bottom (Mike Wilkes); *NHPA* 1 (Laurie
Campbell), 6 (Laurie Campbell), 7 (Lady Philippa
Scott), 17 (Laurie Campbell), 27 (Bryan and Cherry
Alexander), 30 (Rich Kirchner), 39 (Stephen
Krasemann), 42 (Roger Tidman); *Oxford Scientific
Films* 13 (Tony Bomford), 14 (Doug Allan), 19 (Doug
Allan), 21 (Doug Allan), 32 (Daybreak Imagery), 33
(Mark Jones), 45 top (Doug Allan); *Science Photo
Library* 26 (Peter Scoones); *Still Pictures* 8 (Schafer and
Hill), 12 (Alain Guillemont), 16 (Norbert Wu), 25
(Norbert Wu), 31 (Fred Bruemmer), 40 (Thomas
Raupach), 45 middle (Norbert Wu), 48 Mark
Carwardine). Artwork by Michael Posen.

Contents

Meet the Seal

The seal is much more at home in water, than on land. Seals come ashore to rest and give birth to their babies, but on land they are slow and clumsy. In the water, however, they are fast and agile. There are many different kinds of seal. Perhaps the best known is the common seal. It is also called the harbour seal, especially in North America. The common seal lives in the North Atlantic and North Pacific oceans.

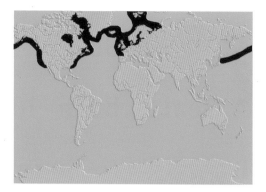

▲ The red shading on this map shows where common seals live.

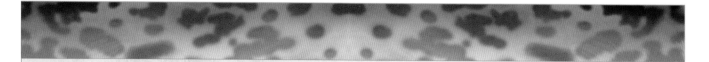

COMMON SEAL FACTS

Male common seals are sometimes known as bulls. Females are called cows. The young are usually known as pups. In some places they are called cubs or calves. The scientific name of the common or harbour seal is *Phocina vitulina*. 'Phoca' is from the Latin word for seal, and 'vitulina' means 'of a calf'.

●

On average, the male common seal is larger than the female. It grows to 1.6–1.9 metres long, from the tip of its nose to the end of its body. A fully-grown, well-fed male weighs 100 kilograms or even up to 150 kilograms. The female common seal grows to a length of 1.4–1.6 metres. She weighs 80–100 kilograms.

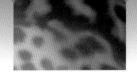

▶ An adult common seal

Ears
The seal has ears and can hear well. But it does not have outer ear flaps like other mammals, such as dogs. There is just a small gap in the fur where the ear is.

Eyes
The seal's eyes are big and dark. They give it very good eyesight, both under the water and above the surface.

Nose and whiskers
The seal has long, pale whiskers to feel in the water and on the seabed. Its snout is small and its nostrils form a V shape.

Front flippers
Instead of arms, the seal has wide, flat flippers. The five fingers are joined together by web-like flaps, and each has a long, black claw at its tip.

Blubber
Under the seal's skin is a thick layer of fat, called blubber. Along with its fur, this helps to keep the seal's body warm in cold conditions.

Rear flippers
The seal's 'legs' are long, flexible webbed flippers. These provide the main pushing power when the seal swims.

Fur
Thick, sleek fur helps to keep in body warmth and makes it easier for the seal to slip through the water.

Common seals

Seals are fairly easy to recognize. They are mammals, like cats, dogs, horses and monkeys. Like other mammals they breathe air, have warm blood and fur or hair, and the babies are fed on mother's milk.

But seals are very different from most mammals as they are adapted to moving and feeding in water rather than on land. Their arms and legs are shaped like flippers to make it easy for them to swim. Their body shape is smooth and streamlined to slip quickly through the water.

▼ Seals usually rest on land, although they rarely sleep and always keep watch for danger.

ARE COMMON SEALS COMMON?

Common seals are called 'common' mainly because they are familiar in Europe and North America, but they are not the world's most numerous seals. There are probably about half a million common seals, compared with over 15 million crabeater seals, which live around Antarctica.

▲ Crabeater seals of Antarctica are among the most numerous large wild animals in the world.

There are 19 different kinds of seal around the world. They all look very similar, apart from their size and the colour of their fur. Common seals live in more places than any other types of seal. They are found in many northern areas, usually along coasts and bays, or at the mouths of rivers.

FLIPPER FEET

Seals belong to the mammal group called pinnipeds, a name which means 'flipper feet'. The pinniped group includes:
- 19 kinds or species of seal (also called true, haired or earless seals),
- 14 species of sea lion and fur seal (also called eared seals),
- the walrus, a single species.

Seal or sea lion?

The only animals that look similar to seals are sea lions. In fact, some people think that seals and sea lions are exactly the same. But there are several differences between them.

◀ Unlike seals, sea lions have flap-like ears and can prop themselves up on their front flippers.

▲ The hooded seal is a medium-sized seal from the far north. It is named after the darker fur over its neck and back, like a 'hood'.

Seals don't have visible ears. Sea lions and fur seals, however, have small ear flaps. These look like curled-up pieces of paper on the sides of their heads.

Seals usually swim by swishing or kicking their rear flippers. Sea lions use their front flippers like oars to 'row' slowly, or they flap them up and down almost like a bird's wings, to 'fly' through the water.

On land, sea lions can prop themselves up on their front flippers, tuck their rear flippers under the body, and waddle along. Seals cannot, and they move by wriggling or 'humping' on their bellies.

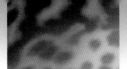

A Seal is Born

A baby common seal is usually born in a remote place, on a quiet beach or sandbank, or among the shingle and rocks of the shore. Most seal pups are born from late spring to the middle of the summer, between May and July.

Some kinds of seal gather together in large, crowded, noisy groups to have their babies. Common seals form smaller, more scattered groups or give birth on their own.

▲ The mother common seal rests but keeps a lookout for danger as she guards her pup.

▶ This is a pup of the grey seal, which is a larger type than the common seal.

BIG BABY

A newborn common seal is 70–100 centimetres long and weighs about 10 kilograms. Compared to the size of the mother, this is quite large. The common seal mother weighs slightly more than a human mother, but the seal pup weighs three times more than a human baby.

The birth takes place very quickly, in just a few minutes. The mother lies still and the baby slips out easily, on to the ground. Its mother licks it clean. The baby's thick, warm fur is similar in colour and pattern to the adult's fur coat. Within minutes the baby seal, or pup, is taking its first meal of rich, creamy mother's milk.

The first days

The common seal pup can wriggle along within minutes of being born and in just a few hours it is learning to swim. The mother stays close to her baby all the time at first. She protects it and helps it to swim, so that it learns not to breathe while under the water.

Seals do not make nests or burrows for shelter. They live out in the open all the time. But the pup is usually born in summer, so the weather is warm and sunny, and the sea is calm.

▼ A young harp seal or 'whitecoat' feeds hungrily on its mother's milk.

GREY SEALS

Grey seals live in many of the same regions as common seals, along North Atlantic coasts. A grey seal is bigger than a common seal, and greyer, with a longer, more pointed head and nose. Grey seal breeding sites, or 'rookeries', are crowded and noisy.

▲ The pale fur of grey seal pups contrasts with the darker colour of their mothers.

The mother feeds or suckles the pup on her milk, every four hours or so, day and night. Feeding takes just one minute. After the first day or two, when the mother has suckled her pup, she goes off to feed for herself, in the sea. The pup is left on the shore. But on the remote coast, there are few other animals that might be a danger.

Growing up

When the common seal pup is only two or three days old, it can already swim well, and stay under the water for two minutes. The mother stays nearby as the pup swims. Sometimes the pup tries to follow her, and she swims slowly so the pup can keep up with her more easily.

As the pup grows, it sometimes feeds from its mother in the water, rather than on land. Its mother floats on her side so that the pup can drink milk from one of the two teats on her belly. A common seal pup rarely has a brother or sister. Mother seals usually produce just one pup each year.

▲ Young seals are soon expert swimmers. This harp seal pup is just two weeks old.

▶ Guarded by its mother, a seal pup nestles in an air-hole in the ice.

If an enemy comes near, the mother opens her mouth to show her sharp teeth, and hisses or growls. She may even gently pick up her pup in her mouth, and dive into the water with it, to escape. The father may be nearby, swimming and feeding. But he does not take any part in caring for his pup.

FAST GROWTH

Common seal pups grow very fast. It takes a human baby about 16 weeks to become twice the weight it was at birth. The seal pup doubles its birth weight in just two weeks.

Learning to Swim

By the time a common seal pup is 10 days old, it is an expert swimmer and diver. It can stay under the water for 10 minutes or more. Its mother still swims nearby, keeping watch, but the young seal doesn't need much help and spends longer in the water each day. When it is tired, it wriggles ashore or 'hauls out' to rest on the sand or a rock.

PREPARING TO DIVE

A seal has hardly any air inside its body when it goes underwater. Air would make it float too well, so it would be difficult to dive for food. The seal also closes its nostrils and the back of its mouth, so that no water can leak in.

▲ The eyes are kept moist by a special fluid while the seal is out of the water. This is why seals sometimes look 'tearful'.

◄ The common seal can see clearly underwater, hear well and also feel precisely with its long whiskers.

Seals swim by pushing themselves through the water with their rear flippers. Each flipper has five long toes, with dark, curved claws at the toe-tips. The seal pulls each rear flipper forwards, then spreads it wide and pushes sideways and backwards. It uses its front flippers to steer, twist and turn in the water.

A seal breathes deeply in and then out before it dives. When it dives underwater, its heart beats much more slowly – only once every five to ten seconds instead of once every second. This helps the seal to save energy and allows it to stay underwater for longer.

On the move

By the time it is three to four weeks old, the seal pup is about three-quarters grown. It has been practising swimming, diving and hunting and can now catch its own food. It no longer needs its mother's milk. This time is called weaning. From now on, the mother and her pup lead separate lives, although they may stay in the same group.

▲ Common seals search for fish among tall fronds of kelp seaweed.

▶ Harp seals remember where their breathing holes are in the ice sheet.

SILENT SEALS

Common seals are probably the quietest of all seals. The pups make a baby-like wailing noise if they are in danger. The grown-ups sometimes cough, grunt or yap like a dog. But often they stay silent for days.

As the common seal pup grows bigger and stronger, it can swim farther. Every few days or weeks, the scattered group of seals it lives with swims 10 or 20 kilometres to a new area, in search of food. Common seals move around like this throughout each year. They follow the sea creatures that they eat, which are also on the move.

Some kinds of seal swim much greater distances. In the North Atlantic Ocean, hooded seals travel hundreds of kilometres northwards each spring, then return the same distance each autumn. These long journeys are called migrations.

Finding Food

Common seals, like all other seals and sea lions, are hunters. They usually find their food on or near the seabed. They keep their eyes open as they dive and they can see well even when the light is dim, many metres below the surface. They chase after fish and other prey, and they also feel in the sand or mud on the seabed with their long, sensitive whiskers. They can hear the swishing of fish prey nearby.

▶ Leopard seals are powerful predators – this one has caught a young penguin.

▼ A seal has four long, sharp teeth, called canines – just like a dog.

Seals have a good sense of smell out of the water. In fact, a mother knows which pup is hers just by its smell. But a seal's nostrils are closed underwater, so it cannot find prey by smell.

Most common seals have about 36 sharp teeth. The teeth near the front of the mouth, called the canines, are extra long, to make it easier to grab prey.

THE FIERCEST SEAL

The leopard seal of the southern oceans is one of the biggest, fastest seals. It grows more than three metres long and weighs over 400 kilograms. This powerful predator eats big fish, squid, seabirds, such as penguins, and other seals.

Diving for dinner

Common seals rarely wander more than about 20 kilometres from the coast. They usually feed in shallow water, less than 100 metres deep. Most dives for food last fewer than five minutes.

Sometimes, if the food is very deep down, a common seal can stay underwater for more than 20 minutes. It may swim down to the seabed, more than 400 metres below the surface. When the seal comes back up, it breathes in and out deeply several times. Damp air and tiny drops of water spray from its nostrils and mouth like a small fountain.

▲ Seals can find food in very dark water, by their sense of touch alone.

Some kinds of seal stay out in the open ocean, far from land, for weeks at a time. They rest for a few hours by floating on the surface, then they dive deep to chase prey such as fish, squid and krill. They might not go ashore for over three months.

▼ The Weddell is one of the biggest seals. A large adult can weigh almost half a tonne.

CHAMPION DIVER

One of the deepest-diving seals is the Weddell seal, from the southern oceans around Antarctica. It can descend more than 500 metres, and stay underwater for over one hour.

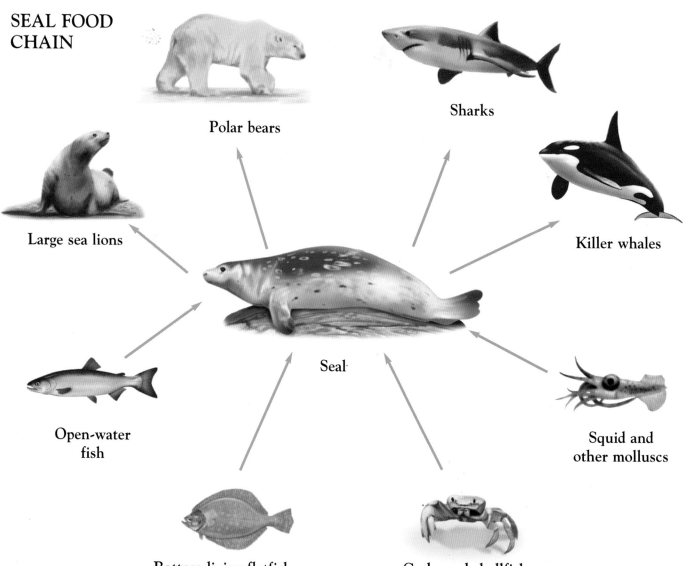

SEAL FOOD
CHAIN

Polar bears

Sharks

Killer whales

Large sea lions

Seal

Open-water
fish

Squid and
other molluscs

Bottom-living flatfish

Crabs and shellfish

Favourite foods

The common seal eats a wide range of sea
creatures. It catches huge quantities of fish,
mostly under 20 centimetres long, which it
swallows whole. These fish include many that
live on or near the seabed, such as flounder and
plaice, but also herring, hake, whiting, sand-eels
and gobies.

▲ The common seal
eats different foods in
different seasons. Few
hunters prey on it.

▶ A common seal
searches for food in
a forest of seaweed
off the coast of
California, USA.

Common seals also catch squid, cuttlefish and small octopuses and crunch up shellfish, such as small crabs and lobsters. Sometimes they dig worms out of the mud on the seabed, or crush sea-snails such as whelks and winkles.

Swimming and diving use up lots of energy, so an adult common seal needs to eat up to three kilograms of food each day. (The average adult person eats about half this much.) Seals mainly feed during the day and at high tide.

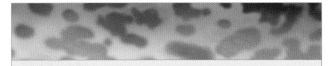

SEALS THAT NEVER SEE THE SEA

Sometimes common seals swim into rivers, chasing fish such as salmon. But some common seals spend their whole lives in fresh water, in lakes and rivers. They are called ungava seals. They live in North America, in the part of Canada called northern Quebec.

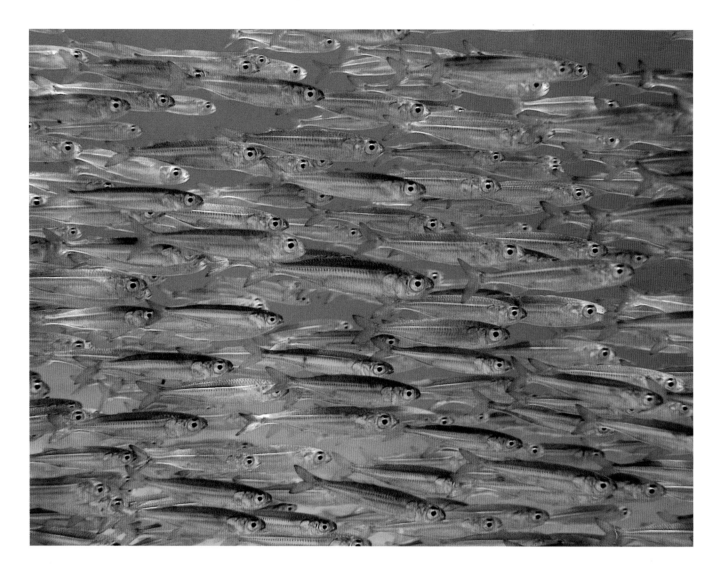

Moving with the seasons

Common seals eat different food, depending on the season. For example, in the North Sea in winter, shoals of haddock swim closer to the coasts and the seals feast on them. In early spring, herring move from the open sea to nearer the shore, especially along the coasts of Norway. This is their breeding season, and the seals have another feast. In the summer, shellfish are the main food in some regions.

▲ Herring move inshore in vast shoals to breed – and seals are waiting for them.

▶ Both male and female walruses have long tusks.

SEALS WITH TUSKS

The walrus is one of the biggest and strangest members of the seal and sea lion group (pinnipeds). Two of its upper teeth grow into tusks up to a metre long. Walruses live in the cold oceans of the far north, and males can weigh up to two tonnes. They eat mainly shellfish.

Common seals are quite big animals, and very strong. They have good eyesight and hearing to detect danger, and a mouthful of sharp teeth to bite enemies. So few predators try to attack and eat them. Common seals can also swim and dive very fast, so even fewer predators can catch them. Most of the common seals that are attacked by bigger hunters are either young pups, or ill or old adults.

Adult Life

Female common seals are fully-grown, and able to breed, at any age from about two to five years. This depends mainly on where they live and how much food they can catch. The males take a year or two longer to become fully grown and ready to breed.

▲ As in common seals, the male grey seal (on the right) is usually larger than the female.

28

It is difficult to tell the difference between a female common seal and a male one. They look very similar, except that the male is usually slightly larger. However, in some kinds of seal there is a much greater difference. The male hooded seal is twice the size of the female, and has a bag-like flap of skin inside his nose that he can blow up like a balloon. He does this both to attract females and frighten off other males.

HOW LONG DO SEALS LIVE?

Female common seals live to 30–35 years of age, and males 20–25 years. This life span is fairly average for seals. However some kinds live much longer. Baikal seals, from Lake Baikal in Russia, often live for more than 50 years.

▼ The male hooded seal blows up a fleshy red 'nose bag' out of one nostril, to attract a partner at breeding time.

Fighting for females

For some kinds of seal, the breeding season is a time for battle. The males rear up to make themselves look tall. Then they roar, push, shove and bite each other. Only the winners can mate with the females. The losers have to wait until the following year. In some cases, the males fight over a small patch of beach, called a territory. Only when a male has a territory, can he become a father.

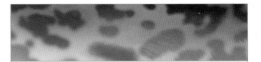

THE BIGGEST BATTLES

Elephant seals are the biggest seals. A full-grown male weighs up to 5 tonnes, as much as a real elephant. These giants roar and clash on beaches at breeding time, to win their territories. The biggest males, called 'beachmasters', mate with the most females. Female elephant seals are much smaller, only one-quarter as heavy as the males.

◄ A male elephant seal bellows out a warning to other males: 'Stay out of my territory!'

▲ Two young male elephant seals practise 'playfighting'. In a few years their battles will be real and very dangerous.

Male common seals do not have such fierce battles. They may push and shove in the water, and roar at each other above the surface and below. They also swim near the females, trying to attract them by twisting and turning in the water. This is called courtship behaviour. Common seals do not form long-term partnerships. Both the males and females mate with several other seals. Mating, like courtship, takes place mainly in the water.

Preparing for winter

In most regions the main mating season for common seals is mid to late summer, as the current pups are growing up and ready to leave their mothers. As the summer ends, common seals often split into smaller groups, which rest on the rocks or sand together. In the water, however, they usually swim and feed on their own. Also about this time, the seals lose their summer fur coats. The hairs fall out as their new, thicker, winter coats grow.

▲ Seals save energy by sunbathing on rocks to keep warm.

▶ The Ross seal of the far south rarely meets other seals of its kind.

SOLITARY SEAL

Some seals stay together in large groups. Common seals form groups too, but the seals don't stay close together, and often come and go on their own. The Ross seal of southern oceans is much more solitary. It usually lives alone, or with just a few others which keep their distance from each other.

Common seals have grey or brown fur, ranging from light to dark. They also have small patches, spots and blotches all over their bodies, including the flippers. When a seal comes out of the water and its fur dries, these colours look lighter. Common seals often arch their bodies as they rest, holding their heads and rear flippers off the ground. Some people think this is to help them to keep cool. Others think that raising their heads higher helps the seals to watch out for danger.

33

Threats

Seals have several kinds of natural threats, including predators and diseases. Occasionally, they are injured or drowned as a result of powerful storms.

The seal's main predators on land are polar bears, the powerful wolverine (a bigger cousin of the stoat and badger), and wild cats, such as the lynx. They are also attacked by large birds of prey, such as sea eagles. Most of these land predators target seal pups, especially while their mothers feed at sea. However, polar bears sometimes creep up and kill adult common seals when they are basking.

▲ The polar bear is one of the common seal's main enemies, in water and on land.

▶ Killer whales patrol the water next to the beach, watching for seals – especially inexperienced pups.

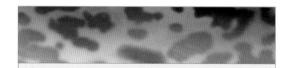

Common seals are slow and clumsy on land. This means that they are more at risk from predators on land than they are in the sea. Sometimes the seals stay on the shore as the tide goes out. This means that the safety of the sea may be dozens of metres away. However, common seals are always on the lookout for predators. As soon as they feel threatened by danger, they hump and wriggle their way towards the waves.

DEATH FROM THE SEA

Sometimes a killer whale swims towards the shore on the surging waves. It crashes on to the beach, grabs a seal in its sharp teeth, heaves itself around, and wriggles back into the sea.

Danger at sea

Common seals are less at risk from predators in the water than on land, because they are such fast swimmers. However, killer whales (orcas) sometimes gather in a group called a pod, to catch a common seal. The killer whales work together to surround the seal, then one moves in to bite and tear its flippers, so that it has less chance of escaping.

FRESHWATER SEALS

Baikal seals live in huge Lake Baikal and its surrounding rivers, in south-east Russia. They are one of the smallest types of seal, and are among the few kinds of seal that live entirely in fresh water. However they face many threats, especially from people.

◀ Steller sea lions are big and strong enough, at almost three metres long, to catch common seals.

▲ Great white sharks prefer warm-blooded prey, like seals, rather than cold-blooded victims such as fish.

Polar bears are a danger in the water as well as on land. Sometimes they hide behind rocks at the edge of a narrow beach and dive in as the seals wriggle into the water. In the North Pacific Ocean a large type of sea lion, called Steller's sea lion, hunts young common seals.

In the sea, there is always the danger of sharks, such as the great white shark. It swims up from the depths to take a huge bite out of any common seal that is not looking out for danger from below.

SEALSKIN

As well as making clothes and boots, traditional peoples used sealskins for many purposes. They can be stretched out over a frame made of branches or bones, to make a tent on land, or a boat such as a kayak for the water.

▲ This Canadian Inuit child has clothes made from the skins of seal and caribou.

Seals and people

For thousands of years, people living near the sea have hunted seals of all kinds. They used almost every part of the seal's body. The meat provided tasty and nutritious food. The fatty blubber under the skin was used for cooking, or burned in lamps for light and warmth. The seal's furry skin made warm coats, clothes and boots. Seal bones and teeth were carved into tools, such as fish-hooks and spearheads, or utensils, such as spoons, as well as ornaments.

Because seals were so useful, they became important in history and folklore. Legends told of famous seal hunts. Pictures of seals were carved on bones, rocks and walrus tusks.

When people followed traditional hunting methods, they only killed as many seals as they actually needed and they used all the different body parts themselves.

▼ These tiny, elegant carvings of walruses are made from walrus tusk 'ivory'.

The human toll

From the early 1700s onwards, seals were hunted in much larger numbers. People shot or clubbed them to death in their thousands. The trade in seal products grew, particularly thick fur coats that were made into fashionable clothes. Seals became big business.

Often, people who rely on fishing do not view seals kindly. Both people and seals want to catch fish. The more fish that seals eat, the fewer there are for people to catch. And the more fish that people catch, the fewer there are for seals to eat. This problem has become very serious in the past fifty years. People have caught so many fish that there are hardly any left in the sea – either for the seals or for themselves.

▶ This Steller sea lion has become caught in a fishing net, and may not survive.

▼ As people catch more fish, there are less for seals to eat. In fact, fish supplies are running out for both seals and people.

Seals are harmed in many other ways. Thousands of seals are trapped underwater in huge fishing nets and drown. Another threat is pollution. People pour wastes, chemicals and other harmful substances into the sea. These get into the seals' bodies and make them ill. Oil spills or slicks get into seals' fur and food and kill them.

SICK SEALS

In the late 1980s, a disease called phocine distemper killed thousands of common seals, especially around the North Sea. The disease returned again in the early 2000s. Perhaps the general level of pollution in the North Sea has made the seals less healthy. This may mean they are no longer strong enough to fight off diseases.

Saving seals

In most parts of the world, people now understand that seals and other animals should be saved for the future. The mass hunting of most types of seal has stopped. Some culling is allowed by hunters who have special licenses. Traditional peoples still catch seals as they have done for centuries.

Seals can be saved in many ways. Less pollution helps not only them, but all sea life. So does setting up marine sanctuaries. These are protected areas of sea and coastline with no hunting, fishing or harm to animals and plants.

▲ Seals are fascinating creatures, and seal-watching from a safe distance is a growing activity.

▶ The Mediterranean monk seal is one of the rarest larger mammals in the world.

Seals are disturbed by people at their haul-out sites, the places along coastlines where they rest and breed. In some areas, sites have been taken over for tourist beaches and watersports, with serious effects. One way of helping is to protect haul-out sites, or even turn them into eco-tourist areas, where people can 'seal-watch' safely.

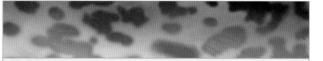

THE RAREST SEAL

There are probably fewer than 500 Mediterranean monk seals left. They are greatly affected by pollution, lack of fish to eat, and also by the tourist sites and holiday beaches spreading around the Mediterranean Sea. The seals now have few places where they feel safe enough to rest and breed.

Seal Life Cycle

1 A mother seal gives birth to a single baby, or pup, about 11 months after mating with a male. The birth takes place on a remote, quiet stretch of coast.

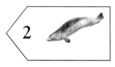 2 A new pup has a thick, warm fur coat, similar in colour to an adult's. Within minutes it takes its first meal of mother's milk, which is very rich, creamy and high in fat nutrients.

 3 In a few hours a young pup can wriggle across the ground, and it is learning to swim in the shallow water. Its mother keeps a watchful eye on it at all times.

 4 At two weeks old, a pup is almost twice as big as it was when born. It still feeds hungrily on its mother's milk, and it is becoming an expert swimmer and diver.

 **5** By four weeks old, a young seal is weaned and it no longer needs its mother's milk. It catches its own food. At first, this is mainly prawns, shrimps, crabs and similar shellfish.

6 Females begin to breed between the ages of two and four years and males a year or two later. Male seals compete to mate with females but seals do not form long-term partnerships.

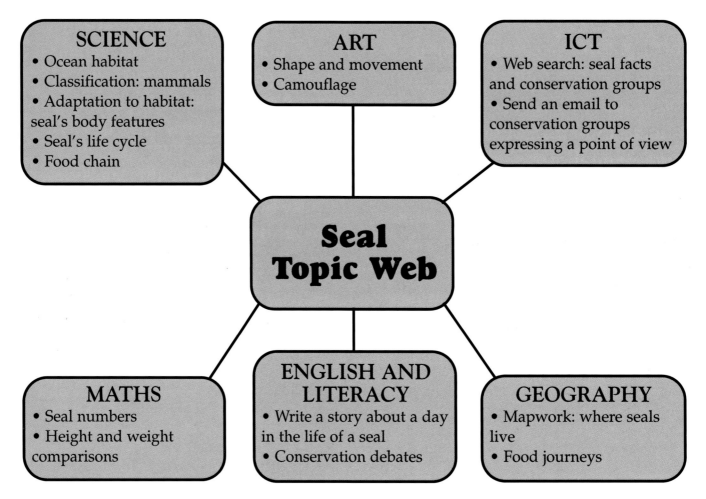

SCIENCE
- Ocean habitat
- Classification: mammals
- Adaptation to habitat: seal's body features
- Seal's life cycle
- Food chain

ART
- Shape and movement
- Camouflage

ICT
- Web search: seal facts and conservation groups
- Send an email to conservation groups expressing a point of view

Seal Topic Web

MATHS
- Seal numbers
- Height and weight comparisons

ENGLISH AND LITERACY
- Write a story about a day in the life of a seal
- Conservation debates

GEOGRAPHY
- Mapwork: where seals live
- Food journeys

Extension Activities

English
- Debate whether seal culling should be allowed.
- Talk about words to describe seals, the way they look and move.
- Write a letter to a Martian describing a seal.

Geography
- Trace a world map from an atlas. Show all the parts of the oceans where seals live.
- Show where seals migrate in order to find food.

Maths
- Make a bar chart showing how long different seals can stay underwater.

Science
- Make a display showing the ways in which seals are adapted to their life at sea.

Art
- Make an ocean frieze, showing different kinds of seal and the other animals that live there.
- Make a poster for a marine sanctuary where you can see seals.

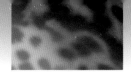

Glossary

Blubber A thick layer of fat under the skin.

Canines Long, sharp pointed teeth near the front of the mouth of hunting animals such as cats, dogs and seals.

Courtship When an animal of one sex, usually male, tries to attract one of the other sex, usually female, for breeding.

Culling The selective killing of some animals in a large group, to keep their numbers down.

Haul out When a water-based animal climbs or wriggles out on to land, usually to rest.

Marine To do with seas and oceans.

Migration A long journey, usually carried out at the same time or season each year.

Pinnipeds The group of mammals that includes all seals, sea lions and walruses.

Predator An animal that kills and eats other animals.

Prey An animal that is killed and eaten by another animal.

Shoal A gathering or group of water animals, especially fish.

Species Animals of one kind or type, who all look similar to each other and can breed together.

Suckle A young mammal drinking milk from its mother's teats.

Territory An area that is occupied and defended by an animal, against others of its own kind.

Weaned When a young mammal has stopped drinking its mother's milk and has moved on to other foods.

Further Information

Organizations to Contact

Seal Conservation Society
The SCS works to protect seals, sea lions and walruses worldwide. It is a non-profit charitable organization set up in 1996. Among its special topics are pollution, setting up protected areas and sanctuaries, and problems with fisheries such as seals tangled in fishing gear. It also deals with culling, hunting and rescuing seals and other pinnipeds.

Seal Conservation Society
7 Millin Bay Road
Tara, Portaferry
County Down
BT22 1QD
United Kingdom

Tel: 028 4272 8600
Email: info@pinnipeds.org

Books to Read

Harpo, the Baby Harp Seal by Patricia Arrigoni, Fred Bruemmer and David White (Travel Pubs Intl, 1995)
Seal Pup Grows Up: The Story of a Harbor Seal by Kathleen Weidner Zoehfeld and Lisa Bonforte (Soundprints Corp Audio, 1994)
Seals (Naturebooks Underwater Life) by Charles Rotter (Child's World, 2001)

Index

Page numbers in **bold** refer to photographs or illustrations.